Helping Your Child Learn Math

with activities for children aged 5 through 13

By Patsy F. Kanter

Edited by Cynthia Hearn Dorfman
Illustrated by Jerry Guillot
with contributions from Brian A. Griffin

U.S. Department of Education
Office of Educational Research and Improvement

GReaT SouRCe®
EDUCATION GROUP
A Division of Houghton Mifflin Company
w w w . g r e a t s o u r c e . c o m
8 0 0 - 2 8 9 - 4 4 9 0

The contents of this book were prepared by the Office of Educational Research and Improvement, U.S. Department of Education. Listing of materials and resources in this book should not be construed or interpreted as an endorsement by the Department or any private organization or business named herein.

Ordering Information

Additional copies of this book are available from Great Source Education Group by calling toll free: 1-800-289-4490 or by fax: 1-800-289-3994. Handling and shipping charges will be added to your order.

Foreword

"Why?"

This is the question we parents are always trying to answer. It's good that children ask questions: that's the best way to learn. All children have two wonderful resources for learning—imagination and curiosity. As a parent, you can awaken your children to the joy of learning by encouraging their imagination and curiosity.

Helping Your Child Learn Math is one in a series of books on different education topics intended to help you make the most of your child's natural curiosity. Teaching and learning are not mysteries that can only happen in school. They also happen when parents and children do simple things together.

For instance, you and your child can: sort socks on laundry day—sorting is a major function in math and science; cook a meal together—cooking involves not only math and science but good health as well; tell and read each other stories—storytelling is the basis for reading and writing (and a story about the past is also history); or play a game of hopscotch together—playing physical games will help your child learn to count and start on a road to lifelong fitness.

By doing things together, you will show that learning is fun and important. You will be encouraging your child to study, learn, and stay in school.

All of the books in this series tie in with the **National Education Goals** set by the President and the Governors. The goals state that, by the year 2000: every child will start school ready to learn; at least 90 percent of all students will graduate from high school; each American student will leave the 4th, 8th, and 12th grades demonstrating competence in core subjects; U.S. students will be first in the world in math and science achievement; every American adult will be literate, will have the skills necessary to compete in a global economy, and will be able to exercise the rights and responsibilities of citizenship; and American schools will be liberated from drugs and violence so they can focus on learning.

This book is a way for you to help meet these goals. It will give you a short rundown on facts, but the biggest part of the book is made up of simple, fun activities for you and your child to do together. Your child may even beg you to do them. At the end of the book is a list of resources, so you can continue the fun.

As U.S. Education Secretary Lamar Alexander has said:

> *The first teachers are the parents, both by example and conversation. But don't think of it as teaching. Think of it as fun.*

So, let's get started. I invite you to find an activity in this book and try it.

Diane Ravitch
Assistant Secretary and
Counselor to the Secretary

Contents

Appendices

Acknowledgments

Introduction

Most parents will agree that it is a wonderful experience to cuddle up with their child and a good book. Few people will say that about flash cards or pages of math problems. For that reason, we have prepared this booklet to offer some math activities that are meaningful as well as fun. You might want to try doing some of them to help your child explore relationships, solve problems, and see math in a positive light. These activities use materials that are easy to find. They have been planned so you and your child might see that math is not just work we do at school but, rather, a part of life.

It is important for home and school to join hands. By fostering a positive attitude about math at home, we can help our children learn math at school.

It's Everywhere! It's Everywhere!

Math is everywhere and yet, we may not recognize it because it doesn't look like the math we did in school. Math in the world around us sometimes seems invisible. But math is present in our world all the time—in the workplace, in our homes, and in life in general.

You may be asking yourself, "How is math everywhere in my life? I'm not an engineer or an accountant or a computer expert!" Math is in your life from the time you wake until the time you go to sleep. You are using math each time you set your alarm, buy groceries, mix a baby's formula, keep score or time at an athletic event, wallpaper a room, decide what type of tennis shoe to buy, or wrap a present. Have you ever asked yourself, "Did I get the correct change?" or "Do I have enough gasoline to drive 20 miles?" or "Do I have enough juice to fill all my children's thermoses for lunch?" or "Do I have enough bread for the week?" Math is all this and much, much more.

How Do You Feel About Math?

How do you feel about math? Your feelings will have an impact on how your children think about math and themselves as mathematicians. Take a few minutes to answer these questions:

- Did you like math in school?

- Do you think **anyone** can learn math?

- Do you think of math as useful in everyday life?

- Do you believe that most jobs today require math skills?

If you answer "yes" to most of these questions, then you are probably encouraging your child to think mathematically. This book contains some ideas that will help reinforce these positive attitudes about math.

You Can Do It!

If you feel uncomfortable about math, here are some ideas to think about.

Math is a very important skill, one which we will all need for the future in our technological world. It is important for you to encourage your children to think of themselves as mathematicians who can reason and solve problems.

Math is a subject for all people. Math is not a subject that men can do better than women. Males and females have equally strong potential in math.

People in the fine arts also need math. They need math not only to survive in the world, but each of their areas of specialty requires an in-depth understanding of some math, from something as obvious as the size of a canvas, to the beats in music, to the number of seats in an audience, to computer-generated artwork.

Calculators and computers require us to be equally strong in math. Their presence does not mean there is less need for knowing math. Calculators demand that people have strong mental math skills—that they can do math in their heads. A calculator is only as accurate as the person putting in the numbers. It can compute; it cannot think! Therefore, we must be the thinkers. We must know what answers are reasonable and what answers are outrageously large or small.

Positive attitudes about math are important for our country. The United States is the only advanced industrial nation where people are quick to admit that "I am not good in math." We need to change this attitude, because mathematicians are a key to our future.

The workplace is rapidly changing. No longer do people need only the computational skills they once needed in

the 1940s. Now workers need to be able to estimate, to communicate mathematically, and to reason within a mathematical context. Because our world is so technologically oriented, employees need to have quick reasoning and problem-solving skills and the capability to solve problems together. The work force will need to be confident in math.

Build Your Self-Confidence!

To be mathematically confident means to realize the importance of mathematics and feel capable of learning to

- Use mathematics with ease;
- Solve problems and work with others to do so;
- Demonstrate strong reasoning ability;
- See more than one way to approach a problem;
- Apply mathematical ideas to other situations; and
- Use technology.

The Basics

You may have noticed that we are talking about "mathematics"—the subject that incorporates numbers, shapes, patterns, estimation, and measurement, and the concepts that relate to them. You probably remember studying "arithmetic"—adding, subtracting, multiplying, and dividing—when you were in elementary school. Now, children are starting right away to learn about the broad ideas associated with math, including problem solving, communicating mathematically, and reasoning.

Kindergarteners are building bar graphs of birthday cakes to show which month has the most birthdays for the most children in the class. Second graders are using pizzas to learn fractions, and measurements are being taken using items other than rulers (for example, the illustrator of this book used his thumb to determine how large the pictures of the pizzas should be in proportion to the size of the words on the activities pages).

What Does It Mean To

- Be a Problem Solver,

- Communicate Mathematically, and

- Demonstrate Reasoning Ability?

A **problem solver** is someone who questions, investigates, and explores solutions to problems; demonstrates the ability to stick with a problem for days, if necessary, to find a workable solution; uses different strategies to arrive at an answer; considers many different answers as possibilities; and applies math to everyday situations and uses it successfully.

To **communicate mathematically** means to use words or mathematical symbols to explain real life; to talk

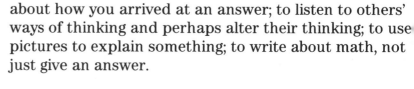

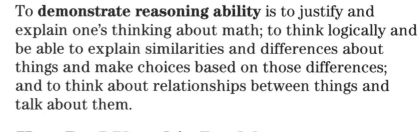

about how you arrived at an answer; to listen to others' ways of thinking and perhaps alter their thinking; to use pictures to explain something; to write about math, not just give an answer.

To **demonstrate reasoning ability** is to justify and explain one's thinking about math; to think logically and be able to explain similarities and differences about things and make choices based on those differences; and to think about relationships between things and talk about them.

How Do I Use this Book?

This book is divided into introductory material that explains the basic principles behind the current approach to math, sections on activities you can do with your children, and lists of resources. The activities take place in three locations: the home, the grocery store, and in transit.

The activities are arranged at increasingly harder levels of difficulty. Look for the circles, squares, and triangles that indicate the level of difficulty. The ● means that a child in kindergarten through 1st grade could probably play the game, the ■ is for those in grades 2 and 3, and the ▲ signals an activity for a child in grades 4 through 8.

The activities you choose and the level of difficulty really depend on your child's ability; if your child seems ready, you might want to go straight to the most difficult ones.

The shaded ● box on an activity page contains the answer or a simple explanation of the mathematical concept behind the activity so that you can explain when your child asks, "Why are we doing this?"

With these few signs to follow along the way, your math journey begins.

Important Things To Know

It is highly likely that when you studied math, you were expected to complete lots of problems accurately and quickly. There was only one way to arrive at your answers, and it was believed that the best way to improve math ability was to do more problems and to do them fast. Today, the focus is less on the quantity of memorized problems, and more on understanding the concepts and applying thinking skills to arrive at an answer.

Wrong Answers Can Help!

While accuracy is always important, a wrong answer may help you and your child discover what your child may not understand. You might find some of these thoughts helpful when thinking about wrong answers.

Above all be patient. All children want to succeed. They don't want red marks or incorrect answers. They want to be proud and to make you and the teacher proud. So, the wrong answer tells you to look further, to ask questions, and to see what the wrong answer is saying about the child's understanding.

Sometimes, the wrong answer to a problem might be because the child thinks the problem is asking another question. For example, when children see the problem 4 + ___ = 9, they often respond with an answer of 13. That is because they think the problem is asking "What is 4+9?", instead of "4 plus what missing amount equals 9?"

Ask your child to explain how the problem was solved. The response might help you discover if your child needs help with the procedures, the number facts, or the concepts involved.

You may have learned something the teacher might find helpful. A short note or call will alert the teacher to possible ways of helping your child.

Help your children be risk takers: help them see the value of examining a wrong answer; assure them that the right answers will come with proper understanding.

Problems Can Be Solved Different Ways

Through the years, we have learned that while problems in math may have only one solution, there may be many ways to get the right answer. When working on math problems with your child, ask, "Could you tell me how you got that answer?" Your child's way might be different than yours. If the answer is correct and the strategy or way of solving it has worked, it is a great alternative. By encouraging children to talk about what they are thinking, we help them to become stronger mathematicians and independent thinkers.

Doing Math in Your Head Is Important

Have you ever noticed that today very few people take their pencil and paper out to solve problems in the grocery, fast food, or department store or in the office? Instead, most people estimate in their heads.

Calculators and computers demand that people put in the correct information and that they know if the answers are reasonable. Usually people look at the answer to determine if it makes sense, applying the math in their heads to the problem. This, then, is the reason why doing math in their heads is so important to our children as they enter the 21st century.

You can help your child become a stronger mathematician by trying some of these ideas to foster mental math skills:

1. Help children do mental math with lots of small numbers in their heads until they develop quick and accurate responses. Questions such as, "If I have 4 cups, and I need 7, how many more do I need?" or "If I need 12 drinks for the class, how many packages of 3 drinks will I need to buy?"

2. Encourage your child to estimate the answer. When estimating, try to use numbers to make it easy to solve problems quickly in your head to determine a reasonable answer. For example, when figuring 18 plus 29, an easy way to get a "close" answer is to think about 20 + 30, or 50.

3. As explained earlier, allow your children to use strategies that make sense to them.

4. Ask often, "Is your answer reasonable?" Is it reasonable that I added 17 and 35 and got 367? Why? Why not?

What Jobs Require Math?

All jobs need math in one way or another. From the simplest thought of how long it will take to get to work to determining how much weight a bridge can hold, all jobs require math.

If you took a survey, you would find that everyone uses math: the school teacher, the fast food worker, the doctor, the gas station attendant, the lawyer, the housewife, the painter.

Math in the Home

This section provides the opportunity to use games and activities at home to explore math with your child. The activities are intended to be fun and inviting, using household items. Please note that the activities for K-1st grade are marked with a ●, the activities for grades 2 and 3 with a ■, and activities for grades 4 through 8 with a ▲.

Remember,

● This is an opportunity for you and your child to "talk math," that is to communicate about math while investigating relationships.

● If something is too difficult, choose an easier activity or skip it until your child is older.

● Have fun!

Picture Puzzle

Using symbols to stand for numbers can help make math fun and easier for young children to understand.

What you'll need

Paper
Pencil
Crayons

Most children feel comfortable drawing pictures. Using pictures to depict numbers helps children learn to count and introduces them to the idea that symbols on a page can represent amounts.

What to do

1. Choose some symbols that your child can easily draw to stand for 1s and 10s (if your child is older, include 100s and 1,000s).

A face could be 10s, and

a bow could be 1s.

2. List some numbers and have your child depict them.

For example:

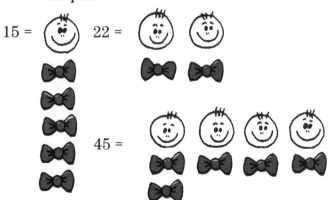

More or Less

Playing cards is a fun way for children to use numbers.

What you'll need

Coin
2 decks of cards
Scratch paper to keep score

What to do

1. Flip a coin to tell if the winner of this game will be the person with "more" (a greater value card) or "less" (a smaller value card).

2. Remove all face cards (jacks, queens, and kings) and divide the remaining cards in the stack between the two players.

3. Place the cards face down. Each player turns over one card and compares: Is mine more or less? How many more? How many less?

This game for young children encourages number sense and helps them learn about the relationships of numbers (more or less than) and about adding and subtracting. By counting the shapes on the cards and looking at the printed numbers on the card, they can learn to relate the number of objects to the numeral.

Problem Solvers

These games involve problem solving, computation, understanding number values, and chance.

What you'll need

Deck of cards
Paper
Pencil

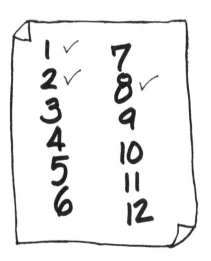

What to do

1. **Super sums.** Each player should write the numbers 1-12 on a piece of paper. The object of the game is to be the first one to cross off all the numbers on this list.

Use only the cards 1-6 in every suit (hearts, clubs, spades, diamonds). Each player picks two cards and adds up the numbers on them. The players can choose to mark off the numbers on the list by using the total value or crossing off two or three numbers that make that value. For example, if the player picks a 5 and a 6, the player can choose to cross out 11, or 5 and 6, or 7 and 4, or 8 and 3, or 9 and 2, or 10 and 1, or 1, 2, and 8.

2.

Make 100. Take out all the cards from the deck except ace through 6. Each player draws 8 cards from the deck. Each player decides whether to use a card in the tens place or the ones place so that the numbers total as close to 100 as possible without going over. For example, if a player draws two 1s (aces), a 2, a 5, two 3s, a 4, and a 6, he can choose to use the numerals in the following way:

30, 40, 10, 5, 6, 1, 3, 2. This adds up to 97.

These games help children develop different ways to see and work with numbers by using them in different combinations to achieve a goal.

Card Smarts

Have your children sharpen their math skills even more.

What you'll need

Deck of cards
Paper
Pencil

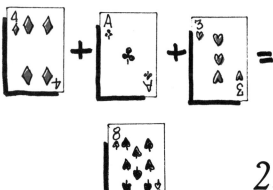

What to do

1. **How many numbers can we make?** Give each player a piece of paper and a pencil. Using the cards from 1 (ace)-9, deal 4 cards out with the numbers showing. Using all four cards and a choice of any combination of addition, subtraction, multiplication, and division, have each player see how many different answers a person can get in 5 minutes. Players get one point for each answer. For example, suppose the cards drawn are 4, 8, 9, and 2. What numbers can be made?

$$4+9+8+2=23 \quad 4+9-(8+2)=3 \quad (8-4)\times(9-2)=28$$
$$(9-8)\times(4-2)=2$$

2. **Make the most of it.** This game is played with cards from 1 (ace) to 9. Each player alternates drawing one card at a time, trying to create the largest 5-digit number possible. As the cards are drawn, each player puts the cards down in their "place" (ten thousands, thousands, hundreds, tens, ones) with the numbers showing. One round goes until each player has 6 cards. At that point, each player chooses one card to throw out to make the largest 5-digit number possible.

3.

Fraction fun. This game is played with cards 1 (ace) - 10, and 2 players. Each player receives one-half of the cards. Players turn over 2 cards each at the same time. Each player tries to make the largest fraction by putting the 2 cards together. The players compare their fractions to see whose is larger. For example, if you are given a 3 and a 5, the fraction 3/5 would be made; if the other person is given a 2 and an 8, the fraction is 2/8. Which is larger? The larger fraction takes all cards and play continues until one player has all the cards.

Players can develop strategies for using their cards, and this is where the math skills come in.

17

Fill It Up

Children enjoy exploring measurement and estimation. Empty containers can provide opportunities to explore comparisons, measurement, estimation, and geometry.

What you'll need

Empty containers in different
  shapes (yogurt cups,
  margarine tubs, juice boxes
  with tops cut off, pie tins)
Rice, popcorn kernels, or
  water
Marker
Masking tape
Paper

What to do

1. Have your child choose an empty container each day and label it for the day by writing the day on a piece of masking tape and sticking it on the container.

2. Discover which containers hold more than, less than, or the same as the container chosen for that day by

filling the day's container with water, uncooked rice, or popcorn kernels; and

pouring the substance from that container into another one. Is the container full, not full, or overflowing? Ask your child, "Does this mean the second container holds more than the first, less, or the same?"

3. Ask your child questions to encourage comparison, estimation, and thinking about measurement.

4. Put all the containers that hold more in one spot, those that hold less in another, and those that hold the same in yet another. Label the areas "more," "less," and "the same."

5. After the containers have been sorted, ask, "Do we have more containers that hold more, hold less, or hold the same? How many containers are in each category?"

The process of predicting, filling the containers, and comparing how much each will hold, gives your child the opportunity to experiment with measurement without worrying about exact answers.

Half Full,
Half Empty

It is helpful to explore whole numbers and fractions through measurement and estimation. Children can see relationships and the usefulness of studying fractions.

What you'll need

Clear container with straight
    sides, that holds at least 4
    cups
Masking tape
Marker
Measuring cup with 1, 1/2,
    1/4, 1/8 cup measures on
    it
Uncooked rice, popcorn
    kernels, or water
Other containers with which
    to compare

What to do

1. Have your child run a piece of masking tape up the side of the container so that it is straight from the bottom to the top.

2. For younger children, use a 1-cup measure. For older children, use a 1/2, 1/4, and 1/8 cup measure. Pour the chosen amount of a substance listed above into the container.

3. Mark the level of the jar on the masking tape by drawing a line with a marker and writing 1 for one cup or 1/2, 1/4, or 1/8 on the line.

4. Follow this procedure until the container is full, and the tape is marked in increments to the top of the container. Now, the jar is marked evenly to measure the capacity of other containers.

5. While filling different containers, ask your child "thinking" questions.

How many whole cups do you think this container will hold?
How many 1/2, 1/4, or 1/8 cups do you think the container will hold?

How many 1/2 cups equal a cup?

How many 1/4 cups equal a 1/2 cup? A cup?
How many 1/8 cups equal a 1/4 cup? A 1/2 cup? A 1/8 cup?

This activity provides a "hands-on" opportunity for children to experience fractions while making connections to the real world.

Name that Coin

Children love to look at coins but sometimes cannot identify the coins or determine their value.

What you'll need

Penny
Nickel
Dime
Quarter

What to do

1. Look at the coins and talk about what color they are, the pictures on them, and what they are worth.

2. Put a penny, nickel, and dime on the floor or table.

3. Tell your child that you are thinking of a coin.

4. Give your child hints to figure out which coin you are thinking of. For example, "My coin has a man on one side, a building on the other."

5. Let your child think about what you have said by looking at the coins.

6. Ask, "Can you make a guess?"

7. Add another clue: "My coin is silver."

8. Keep giving clues until your child guesses the coin.

9. Add the quarter to the coins on the table and continue the game.

10. Have your child give you clues for you to guess the coin.

This guessing game helps young children learn to recognize coins and develop problem-solving and higher level thinking skills.

Money Match

This game helps children count change. Lots of repetition will make it even more effective.

What you'll need

A die to roll
10 of each coin (penny, nickel, dime)
6 quarters

What to do

1. For young players (5- and 6-year-olds), use only 2 different coins (pennies and nickels or nickels and dimes). Older children can use all coins.

2. Explain that the object of the game is to be the first player to earn a set amount (10 or 20 cents is a good amount).

3. The first player rolls the die and gets the number of pennies shown on the die.

4. Players take turns rolling the die to collect additional coins.

5. As each player accumulates 5 pennies or more, the 5 pennies are traded for a nickel.

6. The first player to reach the set amount wins.

7. Add the quarter to the game when the children are ready.

1^s = PENNIES

5^s = NICKELS

10^{s} DIMES

25^s = QUARTERS

Counting money, which involves counting by 1s, 5s, 10s, and 25s, is a challenging skill and usually does not come easily to children until about the third grade.

Money's Worth

When children use coins to play games, it may help them use coins in real life situations.

What you'll need

Coins
Coupons

What to do

1. **Coin clues.** Ask your child to gather some change in his or her hand without showing what it is. Start with amounts of 25 cents or less. Ask your child to tell you how much money and how many coins there are. Guess which coins are being held. For example, "I have 17 cents and 5 coins. What coins do I have?" (3 nickels and 2 pennies.)

2. **Clip and save.** Cut out coupons and tell how much money is saved with coins. For example, if you save 20 cents on detergent, say 2 dimes. Ask your child what could be purchased using the savings from the coupon. A pack of gum? A pencil? How much money could be saved with 3, 4, or 5 coupons? How could that money be counted out in coins and bills? What could be purchased with that savings? A pack of school paper? A magazine? How much money could be saved with coupons for a week's worth of groceries? How would that money be counted out? What could be purchased with that savings? A book? A movie ticket?

Counting money involves thinking in patterns or groups of amounts: 1s, 5s, 10s, 25s. Start these activities by having your child first separate the coins or coupons by types: all the pennies together, all the nickels, all the dimes, all the quarters; the coupons for cereal, the coupons for cake and brownie mixes, the coupons for soap.

In the News

Young children love to look at the newspaper. It is fun for them to realize that there are things for them to see and do with the paper.

What you'll need

Newspaper
Glue
Paper
Scissors
Pencil or crayon

What to do

1. **Newspaper numbers.** Help your child look for the numbers 1-100 in the paper. Cut the numbers out and glue them in order onto a large piece of paper. For children who cannot count to 100 or recognize numerals that large, only collect up to the number they do know. Have your child say the numbers to you and practice counting. Collect only numbers within a certain range, like the numbers between 20 and 30. Arrange the numbers on a chart, grouping all the numbers with 2s in them, all the numbers with 5s, and so on.

2. **Counting book.** Cut out pictures from the newspaper and use them to make a counting book. Page one will have one thing on it, page 2 will have 2 things that are alike, page 3 will have 3 things that are alike, and so on. All the things on the pages have to be the same. At the bottom of each page, write the number of items on the page and the word for the item. Have your child dictate a story to you about what is on the page.

Being able to read and understand the newspaper involves more than just the ability to read the words and understand what they say. It also involves the ability to read and understand numbers.

Look It Up

These activities help children understand how items can be organized and grouped in logical ways.

What you'll need

Newspaper
Paper
Scissors
Glue

Understanding that there is a logical order to the way things are arranged in the newspaper, and in the book of solids, helps show that math skills can be used in organizing written material. Comparing information, such as the sale prices at stores, also helps children see logical relationships that can be applied to writing.

What to do

1. **Section selection**. Show your child that the paper is divided into different sections and explain that each section serves a purpose. Show him that each section is lettered and how the pages are numbered.

2. **Ad adventure**. Provide your child with grocery store ads from the newspaper. Help him see how many items are listed and the prices. Compare the prices at different stores. Ask which store has the best bargain and why. Talk about the difference in prices between items bought at regular price, items on sale, and items bought with coupons. What happens when an item is bought on sale and bought with a coupon?

3. **Solid search**. Look at the store ads or coupons for pictures of all the cylinders, boxes, or cubes you can find. What are their different uses? Paste the pictures on paper and make a "book of geometric solids." Have one page for each solid.

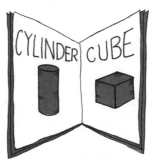

Newspaper Search

Search through the newspaper for mathematical data.

What you'll need

Newspaper

What to do

1. **Numbers in the news.** Find the following things in the paper:

a graph
a number less than 10
something that comes in 2s, 3s, 4s
a number more than 50
the days of the week
a number more than 100
a number that is more than 100 but less than 999
a symbol or word for inches, feet, or yards
a schedule of some kind
a triangle
a weather symbol
a percent sign
sports statistics

2. **List it.** Provide your child with the grocery section of the newspaper in order to make up a list of food that will feed the family for a week and meet a budget of a certain amount of money. Have your child make a chart and use a calculator to figure the cost of more than one item. If the total for the groceries is too great, talk about which items can be eliminated. Could the list be cut down by a few items or by buying less of another item? What will best serve the needs of the family?

3. **For a fraction of the cost.** Give your child a few coupons and grocery ads from the paper. Help your child match the coupons to some of the grocery items in the ad. What fraction of the cost is the coupon? For example, if an item costs 79 cents and the coupon is for 10 cents off, what fraction of the cost can be saved? (About 1/8.) What percent are you saving on the item? (About 12 1/2 percent.)

MANUFACTURER'S COUPON
Save 55¢

One of the main ways people use numbers is for planning. Knowing how to plan how much things will cost before going to the store and how to read schedules and weather information from the paper will help your child understand the world.

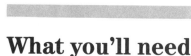

Treasure Hunt

Everyone's house has hidden treasures. There is a lot of math you and your child can do with them.

What you'll need

Buttons
Screws
Washers
Bottle caps
Old keys
Sea shells
Rocks
or anything else you can
    count

What to do

1. Find a container to hold the treasures.

2. Sort and classify the treasures. For example, do you have all the same sized screws or keys? How are they alike? How are they different?

3. Use these treasures to tell addition, subtraction, multiplication, and division stories. For example, if we share 17 buttons among three friends, how many will we each get? Will there be some left over? Or, if we have 3 shirts that need 6 buttons each, do we have enough buttons?

4. Organize the treasures by one characteristic and lay them end-to-end. Compare and contrast the different amounts of that type of treasure. For example, there are 3 short screws, 7 long screws, and 11 medium screws. There are 4 more medium screws than long ones. This may also provide an opportunity to talk about fractions: 7/21 or 1/3 of the screws are long.

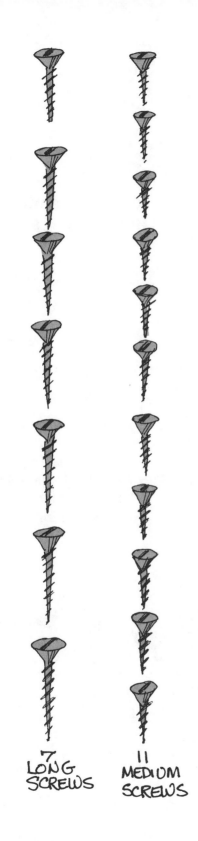

3
SHORT
SCREWS

7
LONG
SCREWS

11
MEDIUM
SCREWS

Finding a container to hold the treasures gives your child practice in spatial problem solving. The treasures may help you to explain the concepts of addition, subtraction, multiplication, and division because they can be moved around and grouped together so your child can count the items.

Family Portrait

Have your child get to know members of your family by collecting information and picturing it on a graph.

What you'll need

Paper
Pencil
Crayons

Graphs help everyone, including adults, understand information at a glance. By looking at the lengths of the lines of heads, your child can quickly see which hair color, for example, is most common.

What to do

1. Choose an inherited family characteristic: hair colors, for example.

2. Count how many people in the family have the different hair colors.

3. Make a graph. For example, if 5 people have brown hair, draw 5 heads side by side to show these five people. Do the same for the other hair colors.

BROWN HAIR

BLACK HAIR

GRAY HAIR

Mathland:
The Grocery Store

The grocery store is one of the best examples of a place where math is real. Since trips to the grocery usually affect everyone in the family, the following activities include various levels of difficulty within the activity. Look for the symbols to determine which parts of the activities are for which ages:

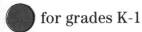 for grades K-1

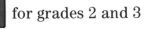 for grades 2 and 3

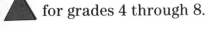 for grades 4 through 8.

All of these activities can take place over many visits to the store.

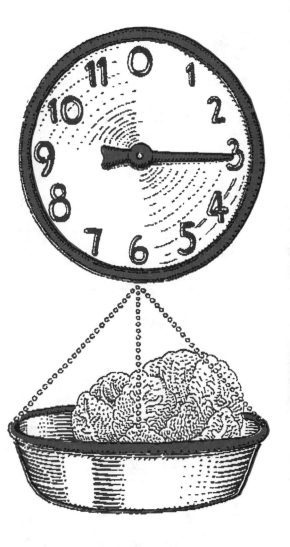

Get Ready

Getting ready to go shopping can help parents and children share their thinking strategies about math with one another.

What you'll need

Paper
Pencil
Coupons (if you use them)

What to do

1. Involve the family in making a list. List each item and mark with checks or tallies to indicate the number needed.

2. Look at the price of an item you bought last week and intend to buy this week. How much did it cost last week? How much does it cost this week? Do you want to

Pay this week's price?

Wait until the price comes down?

Or, stock up if it is on sale?

3. Involve the group in deciding how much milk or juice will be needed for a week. You might decide to estimate by cups, explaining that 4 cups are equal to a quart and 4 quarts are a gallon.

4. If you collect coupons, organize them. Choose the coupons that match the items on the grocery list. Discuss how much money will be saved on various items by using coupons.

Practicing measurement and estimation will help improve your children's ability to predict amounts with accuracy.

Scan It

Shopping is a part of life which really necessitates our being mathematically informed to be good consumers.

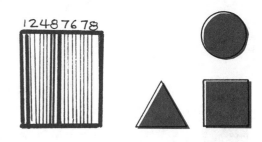

What you'll need

Prices

The ever increasing use of technology in the grocery store puts the burden on you to beware. Your protection lies in having strong mental math skills.

What to do

1. Notice whether the grocery store has prices on the items or whether the pricing is dependent on scanners.

2. If there are no prices on the items, notice the prices listed on the shelves.

3. Assign each child the job of remembering the price of a few items, particularly those listed on sale.

4. Being aware of the prices of items will help you verify that the scanners are working properly and that the total is accurate when you go to check out.

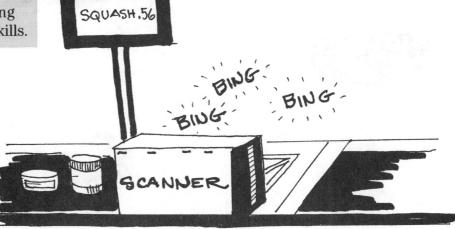

Weighing In

One fun place to try out estimation and measurement skills in the grocery store is the produce section where everyone can have the opportunity to participate.

What you'll need

The grocery scale

What to do

1. Help your child examine the scale. Explain that pounds are divided into smaller parts called ounces and 16 ounces equal a pound.

2. Gather the produce you are purchasing, and estimate the weight of each item before weighing it.

3. Use sample questions to foster thinking about measurement and estimation. You might want to ask your child,

How much do you think 6 apples will weigh? More than a pound, less than a pound, equal to a pound? How much do the apples really weigh? Do they weigh more or less than you predicted? How about the potatoes? Will 6 potatoes weigh more or less than the apples? How much do potatoes cost per pound? If they cost ___ cents per pound, what is the total cost?

Some grocery stores have scales that tell all the answers to these questions, so in that case, estimate using the same procedure to make sure the machines are accurate.

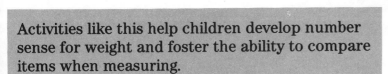

Activities like this help children develop number sense for weight and foster the ability to compare items when measuring.

Get into Shapes

The grocery store is filled with geometric shapes.

What you'll need

Items at the store

CUBE

CONE

CYLINDER

RECTANGULAR PRISM

What to do

1. Show your child the pictures of the shapes on this page before going to the store. This will help to identify them when you get to the store.

2. At the store, ask your child questions to generate interest in the shapes.

   Which items are solid? Which are flat?

   Which shapes have flat sides?

   Which have circles for faces? Rectangles?

   Do any have points at the top?

3. Point out shapes and talk about their qualities and their use in daily life.

   Look to see what shapes stack easily. Why?

   Try to find some cones. How many can you find?

   Look for pyramids.

PYRAMID

Determine which solids take up a lot of space and which ones stack well.

Discuss why space is important to the grocer and why the grocer cares about what stacks well.

Boxes, cans, rolls of toilet paper or paper towels, ice cream cones and cones that hold flowers, plus produce such as oranges, grapes, and tomatoes are all geometric shapes. Recognizing these shapes helps children connect math to the real world.

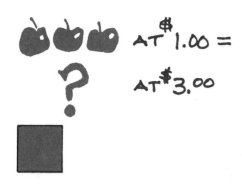

AT $1.00 =

AT $3.00

Check Out

The check out counter is where we commonly think about math in the grocery store. It's where the total is added up, the money is exchanged, and the change is returned.

What you'll need

All the items you intend to buy

One way to make estimating totals easy is to assign an average price to each item. If the average price for each item is $2 and if you have 10 items, the estimate would be about $20.

What to do

1. Have your child estimate the total.

2. Ask, if I have 10 one-dollar bills, how many will I have to give the clerk? What if I have 20 one-dollar bills? 5? How much change should I receive? What coins will I get?

3. Count the change with your child to make sure the change is correct.

STORE

MEAT........6.50
FISH........4.90
CARROTS......1.17
TOMATOES 60
            13.17
TAX   .79

TOTAL 13.96

It's in the Bag

Here's some fun estimation to do with bags full of groceries.

What you'll need

Bags of groceries

This activity exposes children to the experiences of counting items and comparing qualities, as well as to judging spatial relationships and capacity. It shows how to estimate weight by feeling how much the bag weighs, comparing it to a known weight (such as a 5-pound bag of sugar), or weighing it on a scale.

What to do

1. Have your child guess how many objects there are in a bag. Ask: Is it full? Could it hold more? Could it tear if you put more in it? Are there more things in another bag of the same size? Why do some bags hold more or less than others?

2. Estimate the weight of the bag of groceries. Does it weigh 5 pounds, 10 pounds, or more? How can you check your estimate? Now, compare one bag to another. Which is lighter or heavier? Why?

43

Put It Away

Now, the sorting begins as you put away the groceries.

What you'll need

Your bags of groceries
Counter top or table to group
  items on

Sorting helps children
develop classifying and
reasoning skills and the
ability to examine data or
information.

What to do

1. Find one characteristic that is the same for some
of the products. For example, some are boxes
and some are cans.

2. Put all the items together that have the same
characteristic.

3. Find another way to group these items.

4. Continue sorting, finding as many different ways
to group the items as you can.

5. Play "Guess My Rule." In this game, you sort the
items and invite your child to guess your rule for
sorting them. Then, your child can sort the items,
and you can guess the rule.

Math on the Go

In this busy world, we spend a lot of time in transit. These are some projects to try while you are going from place to place.

While you're moving, have your children keep their eyes open for:

- street and building numbers;

- phone numbers on the sides of taxis and trucks;

- dates on buildings and monuments; and

- business names that have numbers in them.

Number Search

The object is to look for numbers around you: on cars, buses, subways, and on foot.

What you'll need

Some type of transportation
  or
A place from which to observe
Paper
Pencil
Ruler

This is a great challenge for family members of all ages, because even young children can learn to recognize numbers.

What to do

1. Create a chart that lists the numbers from 1-50.

2. Write down each number as family members locate that number on a car, a sign, a building.

3. Write down words that have numbers in them such as "one-stop shopping," "two-day service," or "Highway 20."

License Plates

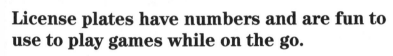

663,218

License plates have numbers and are fun to use to play games while on the go.

What you'll need

License plates
Paper
Pencil

What to do

■ 1. Copy down a license plate. Read it as a number (excluding the letters). For example, if the license is 663M218, the number would be six hundred sixty-three thousand, two hundred eighteen.

■ 2. Find other license plates and read their numbers. Is the number less than, greater than, or equal to yours?

▲ 3. Estimate the difference between your number and another license plate. Is it 10, 100, 1,000, or 10,000?

▲ 4. Record the names of the states of as many different license plates as you see. From which state do you see the most? Which has the fewest? Prepare a chart or graph to show your findings.

These activities encourage reading, recognizing numbers, noticing symbols, writing, counting, and graphing.

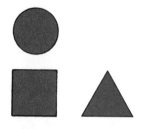

Total It

This is a good game for practicing quick mental computation.

What you'll need

License plates

The problem solving and computation going on in your child's head is very important. It helps your child be creative with numbers.

What to do

●1. Call out the numbers on the license plate.

■2. See who can add the numbers up correctly. What strategies were used? (Were the numbers added by 10's like 2+8; were doubles like 6+6 used?)

▲3. Try different problems using the numbers in a license plate.

For example, if you use the plate number 663M218, ask, "Using the numbers on the plate, can you:

make a 1 using two numbers?	Yes, 3-2=1.
make a 1 using three numbers?	Yes, 6-(3+2)=1
make a 1 using four numbers?	Yes, (6+6)-8-3=1
make a 1 using five numbers?	Yes, 3-[(6+6)-8-2]=1
make a 1 using six numbers?	Yes, 8x2-(6+6)-3=1
make a 2 using 1 number?	Yes, the 2.

48

How Long? How Far?

Many times when you are on the go, you are headed somewhere that requires you be there by a certain time.

What you'll need

Information about how far you're traveling and how long it will take

What to do

1. Ask your children how far they think you are traveling. Yards? Blocks? Miles?

2. Talk about how long it takes to get there. If it is 3:15 now, and it takes 45 minutes to get there, will we make it for a 4:15 appointment? How much extra time will we have? Will we be late?

These types of questions help children see the usefulness of understanding distance and time.

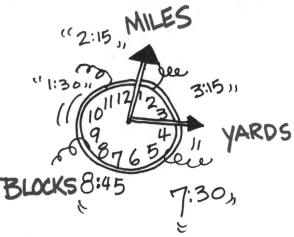

Guess If You Can

When children practice asking questions about numbers, they can develop an understanding of the characteristics and meanings of numbers.

What you'll need

Questions about numbers

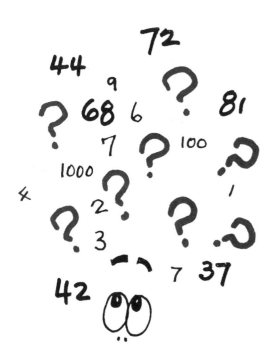

What to do

1. Let your child think of a number between a stated range of numbers while you try to guess the number by asking questions. Here is a sample conversation.

Child: I am thinking of a number between 1 and 100.

Parent: Is it more than 50?

Child: No.

Parent: Is it an even number?

Child: No.

Parent: Is it more than 20 but less than 40?

Child: Yes.

Parent: Can you divide this number up into 3 equal parts?

And so on . . .

2. After you have guessed your child's number, let your child guess a number from you by asking similar questions.

The questions asked demonstrate many different levels of math. They can serve as learning tools for explaining concepts. For example, you can take the opportunity to explain what an even number is if your child does not know.

Parents and the Schools

Here are a few ideas that might help you support a positive math environment in your child's school:

1. Visit the school and see if the children:

- Are actively engaged in math;
- Are talking about mathematics;
- Are working together to solve math problems;
- Have their math work on display;
- Use manipulatives (objects that children can touch and move) in the classroom.

2. Explore the math program with your child's teacher, curriculum coordinator, or principal. Here are some questions you might ask:

- Are there manipulatives in the classroom?
- Are you familiar with the National Council of Teachers of Mathematics standards (see next page)?
- How are the standards being used in this school?
- What can I do to help foster a strong math program where children can explore math concepts before giving the right answer?

3. If you would like to help out, here are some suggestions for parent groups:

- Make games for teachers;
- Help seek out sponsors who believe in a strong math program for the school and who might provide materials and resources;
- Support math classes for families at your school.

4. Keep a positive attitude even if you don't like what you see. Work to improve the math curriculum by doing some of the things mentioned throughout this book.

5. Share this book with your child's teacher.

What Should I Expect from a Math Program?

The National Council of Teachers of Mathematics (NCTM) has recently endorsed standards by which math should be taught in the elementary and middle grade years. The powerful nature of these standards is that they not only have the endorsement of the academic community, but they are also heavily endorsed by corporations. These endorsements, together with the technological advances of our society and the lack of math confidence in our work force, have combined to produce tremendous support for the standards.

These standards make some assumptions about the way math should be taught and what parents might see when visiting the classroom. Here are some examples:

1. Children will be engaged in discovering mathematics, not just doing many problems in a book.

2. Children will have the opportunity to explore, investigate, estimate, question, predict, and test their ideas about math.

3. Children will explore and develop understanding for math concepts using materials they can touch and feel, either natural or manufactured.

4. The teacher will guide the students' learning, not dictate how it must be done.

5. Children will have many opportunities to look at math in terms of daily life and to see the connections among math topics such as between geometry and numbers.

6. Children will be actively involved in using technology (calculators and computers) to solve math problems.

The complete list of standards is available from NCTM, 1906 Association Drive, Reston, Virginia 22091-1593 (1-800-235-7566).

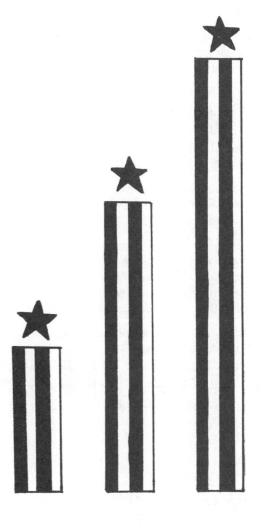

Resources

1. Math for parents:

Burns, Marilyn. *Math for Smarty Pants*. Little, Brown and Company.

Burns, Marilyn. *The I Hate Mathematics Book*. Little, Brown and Company.

Curriculum and Evaluation Standards for School Mathematics. National Council of Teachers of Mathematics. Reston, Virginia

Help Your Child Learn Number Skills. Usborne Parents' Guides, EDC Publishing, 10302 East 55th Place, Tulsa, Oklahoma 74146.

The Learning With Series. Cuisenaire Company, P.O. Box 5026, White Plains, New York 10602-5026, 1-800-237-3142.

Parker, Tom, (1984). *In One Day*. Houghton Mifflin Company.

Reys, Barbara. *Elementary School Mathematics: What Parents Should Know about Estimation*. National Council of Teachers of Mathematics. Reston, Virginia. 10 for $7.50.

Reys, Barbara. *Elementary School Mathematics: What Parents Should Know About Problem Solving*. National Council of Teachers of Mathematics. Reston, Virginia. 10 for $7.50.

Room, Adrian. *The Guiness Book of Numbers*. Sterling Publishing Company, Inc., 387 Park Avenue South, New York, New York 10016-8810.

Stenmark, Virginia Thompson and Ruth Cossey. *Family Math*. Lawrence Hall of Science, University of California at Berkeley, Berkeley California 94720.

Thomas, David A., (1988). *The Math-Computer Connection*. Franklin Watts.

Thomas, David A., (1988). *Math Projects for Young Scientists*. Franklin Watts.
. . .
Math Matters. National PTA and Exxon Foundation. Video tape and pamphlet useful for parent meetings.

The following pamphlets are available from the National Council of Teachers of Mathematics, 1906 Association Drive, Reston, Virginia 22091-1593 (1-800-235-7566). All are priced 20 for $5, 100 for $15.

"Family Math Awareness Activities"

"Help Your Child Learn Math"

"Using Calculators to Improve Your Child's Math Skills"

2. Books for children:

Almost every book you read with your child will offer the opportunity to talk about math, because math is everywhere. Some books lend themselves more to in-depth and specific math discussion. Only a fraction of these books could be listed here.

Anno, Mitsumasa. *Anno's Counting Book*. Thomas Y. Crowell.

Anno, Mitsumasa. *Anno's Counting House*. Philomel Books.

Anno, Mitsumasa. *Anno's Hat Trick*. Philomel Books.

Anno, Mitsumasa. *Anno's Math Games*. Philomel Books.

Anno, Mitsumasa. *Anno's Mysterious Multiplying Jar*. Philomel Books.

Carle, Eric. *The Grouchy Ladybug*. Philomel Books.

Carle, Eric. *1,2,3 to the Zoo*. Philomel Books.

Carle, Eric. *The Very Hungry Caterpillar*. Philomel Books.

Carter, David. *How Many Bugs in a Box?* Simon and Schuster.

Cobb, Vicki and Kathy Darling. *Bet You Can*. Avon.

Cobb, Vicki and Kathy Darling. *Bet You Can't.* Avon.

Conran, Sebastian. *My First 123 Book.* Aladdin Books.

Daly, Eileen. *1 Is Red.* Western.

Dee, Ruby. *Two Ways to Count to Ten.* Holt.

Demi. *Demi's Count the Animals 123.* Grosset and Dunlap.

Feelings, Muriel. *Moja Means One: Swahili Counting Book.* Dial.

Grayson, Marion. *Let's Count.* Robert B. Luce, Inc.

Grayson, Marion. *Count Out.* Robert B. Luce, Inc.

Hoban, Tana. *Circles, Triangles, and Squares.* MacMillan Publishing Company, Inc.

Hoban, Tana. *Count and See.* Macmillan Publishing Company, Inc.

Hoban, Tana. *Is It Rough, Is It Smooth, Is It Bumpy?* Macmillan Publishing Company, Inc.

Hudson, Cheryl. *Afro-Bets 123 Book.* Just Us Productions.

Hutchins, Pat. *The Doorbell Rang.* Greenwillow Books.

Hutchins, Pat. *One Hunter.* Greenwillow Books.

Jones, Carol. *This Old Man.* Houghton Mifflin Company.

Keats, Ezra Jack. *Over in the Meadow.* Scholastic.

Kitchen, Bert. *Animal Numbers.* Dial.

Kredenser, Gail. *One Dancing Drum.* Phillips.

Lionni, Leo. *Numbers To Talk About.* Pantheon Books.

Marley, Deborah. *Animals One to Ten.* Raintree.

McMillan, Bruce. *Counting Wildflowers.* Lothrop, Lee & Shepard Books, Inc.

McMillan, Bruce. *One, Two, One Pair.* Scholastic.

Nolan, Dennis. *Monster Bubbles.* Prentice Hall.

Pluckrose, Henry. *Know about Counting.* Franklin Watts.

Pomerantz, Charlotte. *The Half-Birthday Party.* Clarion Books.

Ross, H.L. *Not Counting Monsters.* Platt and Munk.

Schwartz, David M. *How Much Is a Million?* Lothrop, Lee & Shepard Books, Inc.

Schwartz, David M. *If You Made a Million.* Lothrop, Lee & Shepard Books, Inc.

Tafuri, Nancy. *Who's Counting?* William Morrow & Co.

Testa, Fulvio. *If You Take a Pencil.* Dial.

Viorst, Judith. *Alexander Who Used To Be Rich Last Sunday.* Atheneum.

Vogel, Ilse-Margret. *1 Is No Fun, But 20 Is Plenty!* Atheneum.

Ziefert, Harriet. *A Dozen Dizzy Dogs.* Random House.

3. Magazines and periodicals:

Dynamath. Scholastic. Available from the school division. Filled with many different activities that involve all strands of math. Children in grade 5 particularly like this. Nine publications are sent each school year. $5.00 for the subscription.

Games Magazine, P.O. Box 10147, Des Moines, Iowa 50347. The adult version of Games Junior (see below). Older children may prefer this to *Games Junior.*

Games Junior, P.O. Box 10147, Des Moines, Iowa 50347. A challenging but fun magazine of all different kinds of games that give children hours of "brain workouts." Appropriate for ages 7 and up.

Math Power. Scholastic. Available from the school division. Exciting and inviting, this magazine is filled with many activities that involve all types of math. Good for grades 3 and 4. Nine publications are sent each school year for $5.00.

Puzzlemania. Highlights, P.O. Box 18201, Columbus, Ohio 43218-0201. Includes puzzles involving words, logical thinking, hidden pictures, spatial reasoning, etc. The cost is about $7.50 per month.

Zillions. Consumer Reports, P.O. Box 54861, Boulder, Colorado 80322. Children's version of Consumer Reports. Shows math in the real world and offers children the opportunity to see how gathering data and information can lead to good decisionmaking. The cost is approximately $2.75 per issue.

Acknowledgments

This book was made possible with help from the following people: Phil Demartini, Headmaster, St. Francis School, Goshen, Kentucky; Janet G. Gillespie, Teacher, Woodlawn Elementary School, Portland, Oregon; David Kanter; Sharon Nelson, Principal, Lower School, Isidore Newman School, New Orleans, Louisiana; Kathy Rabin, Teacher, Isidore Newman School; and Annette Raphel, Curriculum Coordinator, Milton Academy, Milton, Massachusetts.

Others who reviewed early drafts or provided information and guidance include: Iris Carl, Past President, National Council of Teachers of Mathematics; Mary Connolly, Marketing Manager, Elementary Mathematics, DC Heath; Julie Fisher, Visiting Mathematics Educator, National Council of Teachers of Mathematics; Vera M. White, Principal, Jefferson Junior High School, Washington, D.C.; and many people in the U.S. Department of Education.

Special thanks go to Leo and Diane Dillon for their advice on how to work with illustrators and to Alison Goldstein and Emily Dorfman, two Maryland third graders who marked the manuscript for color overlays. Appreciation is also expressed to Nathan and Julie Kanter for testing many of the activities contained in this book.

Patsy F. Kanter is Assistant Principal/Curriculum Coordinator at the Isidore Newman Lower School in New Orleans, Louisiana. She is also an instructor of family math and a consultant for the Louisiana Children's Museum. She has been an elementary school mathematics teacher, and she founded the Newman Math Institute at Newman School. She is the author, with Janet Gillespie, of *Every Day Counts* and *Math Every Day* and has written articles on mathematics for professional magazines. She has a B.A. from Newcomb College, and, in listing her academic credentials, she credits her mother, Louise Hirsch Friedler, as being her first teacher, "who always tried to make learning interesting for me."

Jerry Guillot is the art teacher for Isidore Newman Lower School in New Orleans, Louisiana, where he has taught for the past 24 years. He has a B.A. from Lousiana State University and received his teaching certification from Tulane University. He has taught classes and workshops on elementary art for both college students and private organizations. He is also a graphic artist for a New Orleans company.

Brian A. Griffin (pages 10, 11, 30, 35, 45, 46) is a designer for the *San Jose Mercury News*, San Jose, California. He was formerly the Art Director of *Kids Today*, a weekly children's newspaper published by Gannett Co., Inc. He has won awards from the Society of Newspaper Design, *PRINT* Regional Design Annual, and the Art Director's Club of Metropolitan Washington.